For Ryan
—L.K.

For Rick
—J.G.

Clarion Books is an imprint of HarperCollins Publishers.

It Belongs to the World: Frederick Banting and the Discovery of Insulin
Text copyright © 2024 by Lisa Katzenberger
Illustrations copyright © 2024 by Janina Gaudin
All rights reserved. Manufactured in Italy. No part of this book may be used or reproduced in any manner whatsoever without
written permission except in the case of brief quotations embodied in critical articles and reviews. For information address
HarperCollins Children's Books, a division of HarperCollins Publishers, 195 Broadway, New York, NY 10007.
www.harpercollinschildrens.com

Library of Congress Control Number: 2023948809
ISBN 978-0-06-323667-7

The artist used Adobe Photoshop to create the digital illustrations for this book.
Typography by Marisa Rother
24 25 26 27 28 RTLO 10 9 8 7 6 5 4 3 2 1

First Edition

IT BELONGS TO THE WORLD

Frederick Banting and the Discovery of Insulin

WRITTEN BY
Lisa Katzenberger

ILLUSTRATED BY
Janina Gaudin
aka Miss Diabetes

CLARION BOOKS
An Imprint of HarperCollinsPublishers

Frederick Banting was born in a farmhouse in the winter of 1891. As a young boy, he started his days caring for animals before trekking to school.

His school was far away from his farmstead and his siblings were much older than him. Out in the quiet Canadian countryside, the world could feel lonely.

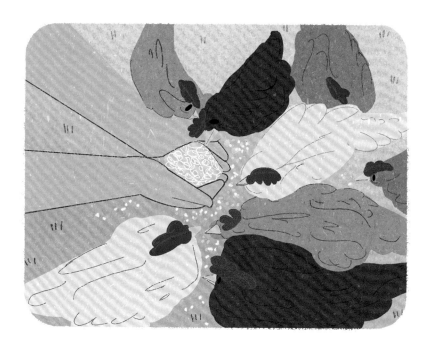

When Frederick came home each day, he fed chickens and tended to horses. When he wasn't working, he would ice-skate on the frozen river, ride through town on his horse, or listen to his father read.

Frederick was shy, but his parents taught him to work hard and help others. He felt most comfortable caring for animals on the farm. When they got sick or died, he was curious to discover what had harmed them so he could help.

Frederick loved learning. Still, when it was time for college, he struggled. He dropped out after he failed his first year and returned to work on the family farm.

The animals continued to spark his curiosity about curing illness. Frederick re-enrolled in college to study surgery, and finally his schoolwork flourished.

While he was away at college, one of his childhood friends died from a disease called diabetes. Frederick was filled with grief, and more determined than ever to help others.

The day after he graduated college, Frederick joined the army to fight in the First World War. In the trenches, the world was dark and frightening. But he always took care of his fellow soldiers, even when he was injured himself.

When he left the army, Frederick opened his own medical practice.
He waited for patients to knock on his door, but they never did.

After a month of working as a doctor, Frederick had made only four dollars! So he took a university teaching job to make money and share his medical knowledge with students.

While preparing for a class about diabetes, Frederick read an article about the pancreas, an organ in the abdomen that processes glucose, which is sugar from food that turns into energy.

People who have diabetes are missing a hormone, a messenger chemical that sends information to parts of the body. The hormone allows the pancreas to do its job. Without it, sugar builds up in the bloodstream instead of turning into energy, which can make diabetics very sick.

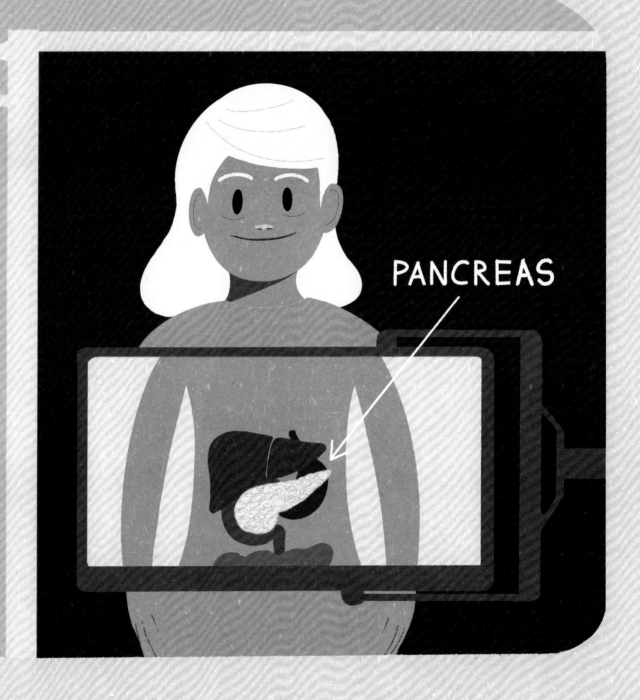

PANCREAS

At the time, there was no treatment
for this disease. Most diabetics died.

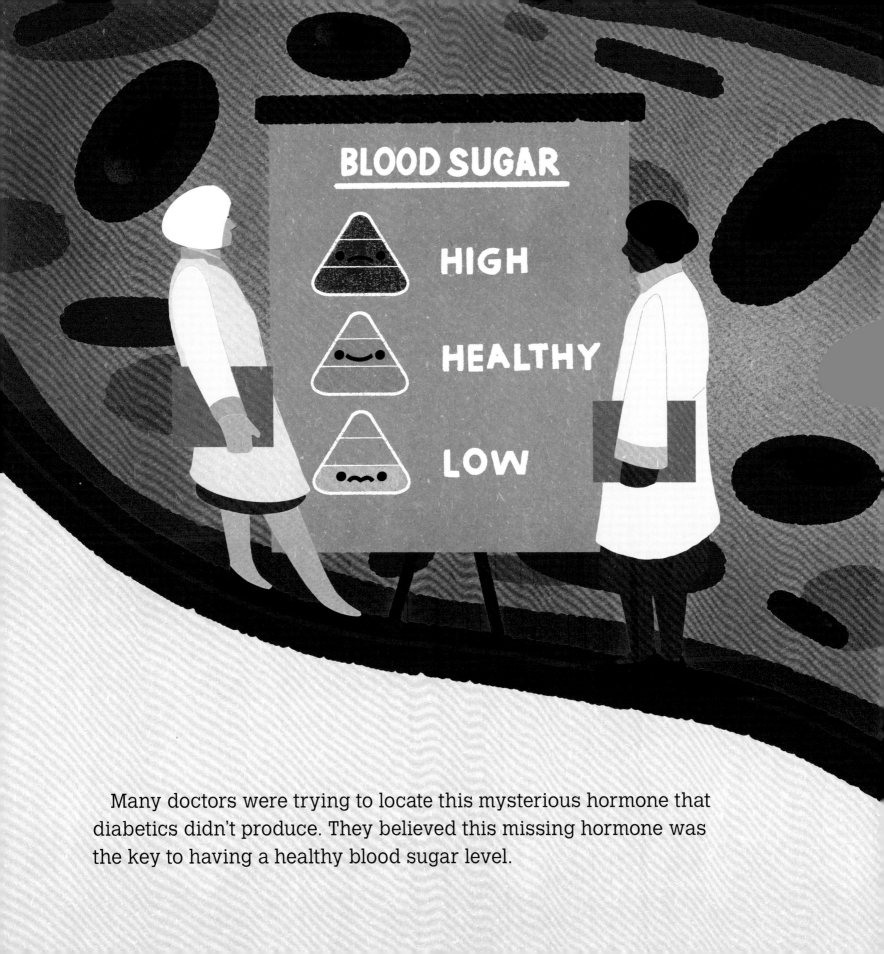

Many doctors were trying to locate this mysterious hormone that diabetics didn't produce. They believed this missing hormone was the key to having a healthy blood sugar level.

But no one knew how to find it.

Later that night, Frederick had an idea so brilliant, he jolted from his sleep.

He thought of a new way to capture this hormone from a healthy pancreas and study it. If it worked, diabetics would finally have the medicine they needed to stay alive.

Frederick talked about his idea with friends the very next day. One friend referred Frederick to J. J. R. Macleod at the University of Toronto for help. Macleod was uncertain about the experiment, but Frederick was persistent.

Macleod finally provided a small lab and an assistant, medical student Charles Best. The lab was old, dirty, and hot. Frederick and Charles cleaned the dingy floor on their hands and knees.

To perform his experiment, Frederick worked with dogs, removing their pancreas to make them diabetic. Then Frederick and Charles would create an extract from the pancreas that would be safe to inject into the dogs.

Frederick hypothesized that the injection would lower the diabetic dog's blood sugar levels.

And he was right!
The injection of the
pancreatic hormone allowed
cells to accept the energy from
the sugar in the bloodstream.

However, the results were not consistent. Sometimes the medicine was too strong, sometimes it was too weak.

Yet Frederick pushed on.

He hired chemist James Collip to help clean the pancreatic extract. Over and over, day after day, they performed their experiments. Analyzing and testing, testing and analyzing. Little by little, the dogs began to improve.

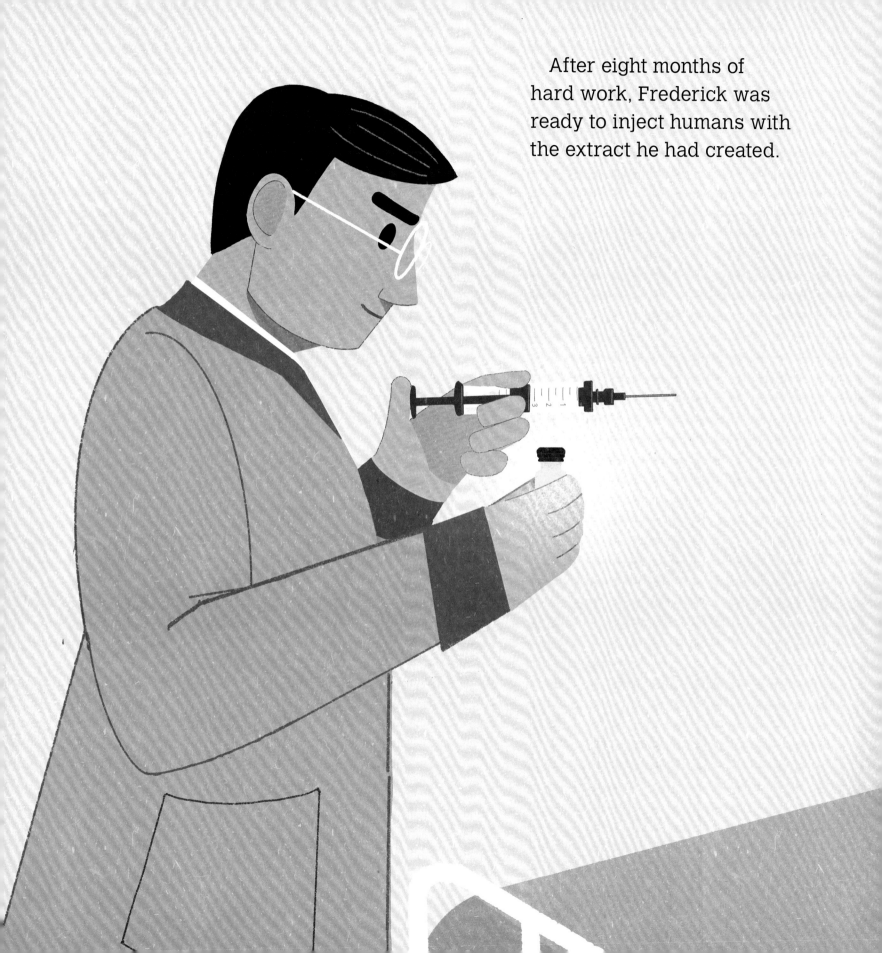

After eight months of hard work, Frederick was ready to inject humans with the extract he had created.

Fourteen-year-old Leonard Thompson—weak, pale, and losing his hair—was the first patient. After the initial dose, Leonard didn't get any better.

As Frederick watched Leonard get sicker, drifting in and out of a coma, his hope faded.

But Frederick was determined. The team worked night and day to make the extract just right. They analyzed and tested, tested and analyzed.

Twelve days later, Leonard received another injection from a fresh batch of the hormone. His sugar levels dropped significantly—his body was getting energy from his food!

Frederick's plan was a success. His heart soared. Frederick and his team wrote an article about their discovery.

It was the first time they publicly named this mystery hormone—insulin.

As Frederick treated more children with insulin, he found that light came into their eyes after just the first injection. He knew they could now play, go back to school, and live active lives as happy, healthy children.

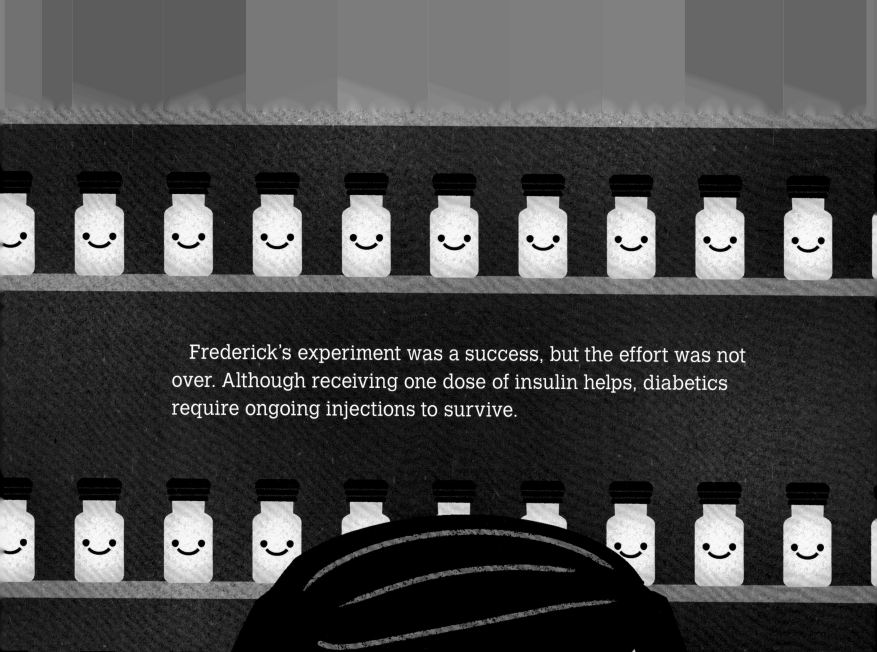

Frederick's experiment was a success, but the effort was not over. Although receiving one dose of insulin helps, diabetics require ongoing injections to survive.

He was offered hundreds, thousands, even a million dollars to explain how to create this miracle medicine. But Frederick decided to sell the instructions for making insulin for just *one dollar*!

Why did Frederick do this? He had a powerful answer.

"Insulin does not belong to me,"
he said. "It belongs to the world."

One hundred years after the discovery of insulin, there is
still no cure for diabetes. But millions of people support World
Diabetes Day each year on November 14, Frederick's birthday.

Access to Insulin

Even today, some diabetics have challenges getting the medicine they need to survive. All people with type 1 diabetes, and some with type 2 diabetes, need insulin. If they don't have it, they will die. But despite Frederick's wishes, insulin is expensive. One vial can cost up to $300 in the US, which is about a hundred times what it costs to make it. Many people with diabetes require two to three vials of insulin a month, which means they must pay up to $10,000 a year just to stay alive.

Health insurance companies may pay for a portion of the cost of insulin, but people without insurance must pay the full price. People who can't afford it will often ration their insulin—which means they take less than they need. With less insulin, a diabetic's blood glucose will remain high and that can hurt the body. Long-term effects of high blood glucose levels include damage to the eyes, nerves, kidneys, and feet. There is also a risk of going into diabetic ketoacidosis, which can be deadly.

Today, there are many people who advocate for more affordable insulin for all, following Frederick's belief that insulin belongs to the world.

How Insulin Works

When a person has type 1 diabetes, their pancreas doesn't create insulin. Insulin is a hormone, or a chemical messenger, that cues the body's cells to capture the glucose, or sugar, from food. When this happens, glucose gives the body energy. But without insulin, cells can no longer receive sugar from food. The sugar has nowhere to go, so it builds up in the bloodstream, which is dangerous. Injecting insulin into the body ensures that blood sugar levels remain safe and healthy.

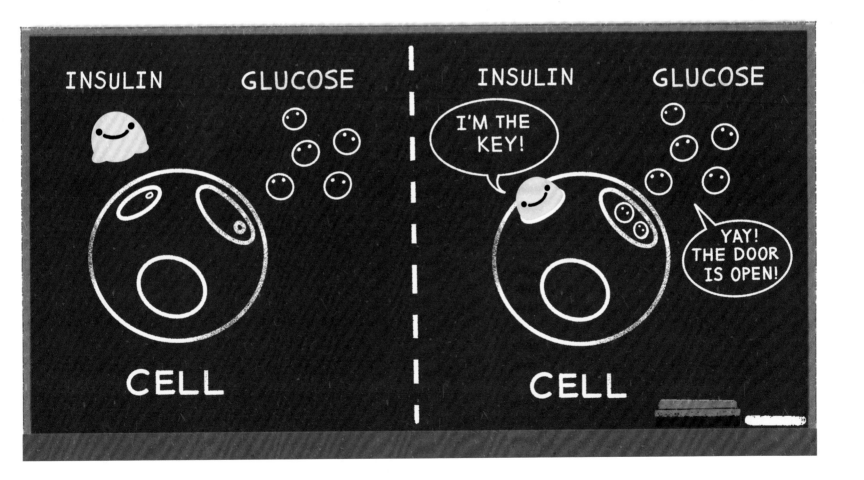

Author's Note

My family has a special connection to Dr. Banting. My son Ryan was diagnosed with type 1 diabetes when he was seven years old. That summer, I noticed Ryan was looking thinner than usual. He also started going to the bathroom a lot. When he woke up in the morning, his breath had a fruity odor.

The final clue about what was happening came during an outdoor Cub Scouts event. It was raining and the boys were gathered under a pavilion eating cupcakes. But Ryan didn't want a cupcake. He was so desperately thirsty that instead of having a treat, he wanted to walk to a water fountain through the pouring rain. All these things—excessive thirst and urination, fruity breath, and weight loss—were signs of type 1 diabetes. We visited Ryan's doctor, who sent us to the emergency room so Ryan could receive insulin treatment right away.

Ryan now has a pump attached to his body that gives him the insulin he needs. He also wears a continuous glucose monitor that gives us his blood sugar readings every five minutes.

While Ryan's chronic illness will be with him all his life, he can do anything other kids can do. He loves to swim, hang out with friends, and play video games. He can eat anything he wants, too—even cupcakes!

While there is currently no cure for diabetes, we hope that Ryan will see one in his lifetime. In the meantime, our family is very grateful to Dr. Frederick Banting and his team for the discovery of insulin.

Illustrator's Note

I was diagnosed with type 1 diabetes in 1994, when I was thirteen years old.

I was always thirsty, going to the toilet a lot, and had lost a lot of weight. I actually guessed before I was diagnosed that I must have type 1 diabetes. I recognized my symptoms because I had just read *The Babysitters Club: The Truth about Stacey*.

As a young teen, this new life with a chronic disease was overwhelming. It soon dawned on me that my life would always depend on a tiny vial of liquid called insulin.

I've always wanted to be an illustrator. One day I was talking with my diabetes nurse about pursuing illustration as a career. She asked if there was anything creative I could do that could help people living with type 1 diabetes. That's when I started making illustrations and comics about my life with type 1 diabetes, because I wanted people to know they are not alone in their journey with this chronic disease.

It was while I was creating comics and an animation about Dr. Frederick Banting that I learned about how miraculous the discovery of insulin was. Dr. Banting was determined that every person with diabetes should have access to insulin. His most famous quote, "Insulin does not belong to me, it belongs to the world," is why I think of him as the first #insulin4all advocate. At present, one in two people in the world do not have access to insulin. Dr. Banting is a constant inspiration to me in my own advocacy and artwork to make insulin accessible to everyone.

It is truly an honor to illustrate my hero, Dr. Frederick Banting!

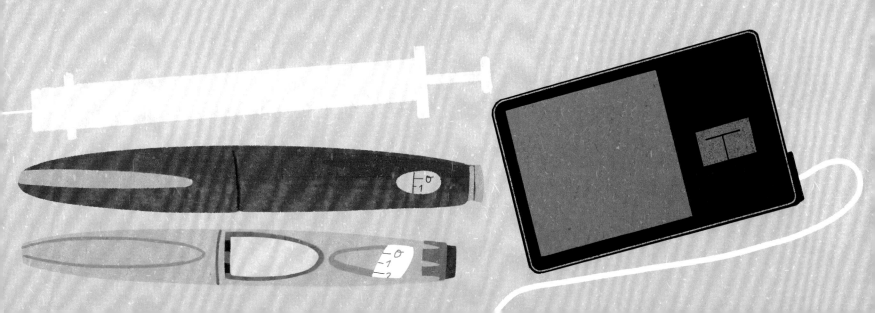

Glossary

- **beta cells**—The cells in the pancreas that create insulin

- **glucose**—The sugar (energy) in our blood. Glucose either comes from food you eat or is produced by your body's liver.

- **hormone**—A messenger chemical that sends information to specific parts of your body

- **hyperglycemia**—Very high blood sugar, which occurs when your body does not have enough insulin

- **hypoglycemia**—Very low blood sugar, which occurs when your body produces too much insulin

- **immune system**—A system of cells, tissues, and organs that protect the body from germs and infections

- **insulin**—A hormone in the body that allows the body's cells to accept the glucose (sugar) from food for energy. It's the key that opens the door to our cells and lets the glucose in.

- **pancreas**—A part of the body, located behind the stomach, that produces insulin

- **type 1 diabetes**—An autoimmune disease where the body's immune system destroys the beta cells, preventing the pancreas from producing insulin

- **type 2 diabetes**—A disease where a person's body does not make enough insulin or cannot use it properly

Fred & Marjorie: A Doctor, a Dog, and the Discovery of Insulin, written by Deborah Kerbel, illustrated by Angela Poon (Owlkids, 2021)

Diabetes Doesn't Stop Maddie!, written by Sarah Glenn Marsh, illustrated by Maria Luisa Di Gravio (Albert Whitman & Company, 2020)

Just Ask! Be Different, Be Brave, Be You, written by Sonia Sotomayor, illustrated by Rafael López (Philomel Books, 2019)

Shia Learns about Insulin, written by Shaina Hatchell, illustrated by Candice Bradley (The Brown Skin & Insulin Collective, 2022)

Teddy Talks: A Paws-itive Story about Type 1 Diabetes, written by Vanessa Messenger, illustrated by Emma Latham (Messenger Publishing, 2021)

Selected Bibliography

Banting, Frederick. "Diabetes and Insulin." Nobel lecture delivered at Stockholm, Sweden, September 15, 1925.

Banting, Frederick. "The Early Story of Insulin." Excerpt from speech delivered at Lilly Research Laboratories, Indianapolis, IN, October 11, 1934.

Banting, Frederick. *Insulin.* Philadelphia: J.B. Lippincott Company, 1924.

Banting, Frederick, and Charles Best. "The internal secretion of the pancreas." *Journal of Laboratory and Clinical Medicine*, vol. VII (February 1922).

Banting, Frederick et al. "The effect produced on diabetes by extracts of pancreas." Paper presented at the annual meeting of the Association of American Physicians, Washington, DC, 1922.

Bliss, Michael. *Banting: A Biography.* Toronto: University of Toronto Press, 1993.

Bliss, Michael. *The Discovery of Insulin*, Twenty-fifth Anniversary Edition. Chicago: University of Chicago Press, 2007.

University of Toronto Libraries. "The Discovery and Early Development of Insulin." Online library collection. https://insulin.library.utoronto.ca.